MORE HIDE & SPEAK
FRENCH

Catherine Bruzzone and Sam Hutchinson
French text: Marie-Thérèse Bougard
Illustrated by Louise Comfort

b small publishing

Ma maison - My house

1	Papa est dans **la cuisine**.	1	Dad is in **the kitchen**.
2	Je lis dans **le salon**.	2	I am reading in **the sitting room**.
3	**Ma chambre** est petite.	3	My **bedroom** is small.
4	Il y a deux **toilettes**.	4	There are two **toilets**.
5	**La salle de bain** est grande.	5	**The bathroom** is big.
6	**Le plafond** est haut.	6	**The ceiling** is high.
7	Maman descend **l'escalier**.	7	Mum is coming down **the stairs**.
8	**Le jardin** est derrière la maison.	8	**The garden** is behind the house.
9	Il y a un oiseau sur **le toit**.	9	There is a bird on **the roof**.

la cuisine

la kwee-zeen

le salon

ler sah-loh

la chambre

lah shombr'

les toilettes

leh twah-let

la salle de bain

lah sal-der-bah

le plafond

ler plaf-oh

l'escalier

less-kalee-eh

le jardin

ler shar-dah

le toit

ler twah

Pendant la semaine - During the week

1	**Lundi**, je vais à l'école.	1	On **Monday**, I go to school.
2	**Mardi**, je fais de la natation.	2	On **Tuesday**, I go swimming.
3	**Mercredi**, je vais au cinéma.	3	On **Wednesday**, I go to the cinema.
4	**Jeudi**, je joue au foot.	4	On **Thursday**, I play football.
5	**Vendredi**, je regarde la télé.	5	On **Friday**, I watch television.
6	**Samedi**, je vais chez mon ami.	6	On **Saturday**, I go to my friend's house.
7	**Dimanche**, je visite ma grand-mère.	7	On **Sunday**, I visit my grandmother.
8	**Aujourd'hui**, je prépare le dîner.	8	**Today**, I am cooking supper.
9	**Demain**, je vais à une fête.	9	**Tomorrow**, I am going to a party.

Les jours de la semaine - Days of the week

lundi
lern-dee

mardi
mar-dee

mercredi
mair-kr'-dee

jeudi
sher-dee

vendredi
vondr'-dee

samedi
samdee

dimanche
dee-moh-nsh

aujourd'hui
oh-shoor-dwee

demain
der-mah

5

Visiter un ami - Visiting a friend

1 **Bonjour**, Marie. Entre.

2 **Oui**, j'aime ce jeu d'ordinateur.

3 **Non**, je n'aime pas ce CD.

4 Je peux avoir quelque chose à boire, **s'il vous plaît**?

5 **Voilà**. Attention!

6 Oups, **pardon**!

7 **Ça va**. Ne t'inquiète pas.

8 **Au revoir**, reviens demain.

9 **Merci**. À demain!

1 **Hello**, Mary. Come in.

2 **Yes**, I like this computer game.

3 **No**, I don't like this CD.

4 Can I have a drink, **please**?

5 **Here you are**. Be careful!

6 Oops, **sorry**!

7 **That's okay**. Don't worry.

8 **Goodbye**, come again tomorrow.

9 **Thanks**. See you tomorrow!

bonjour
boh-shoor

oui
wee

non
noh

s'il vous plaît
seel-voo-pleh

voilà
vwah-lah

pardon
par-doh

ça va
sa-vah

au revoir
oh-r'-vwah

merci
mair-see

Au parc - At the park

1. **La fille** est sur **la balançoire**.
2. Guillaume et Annie sont sur **la balançoire**.
3. Il y a un chien dans **l'allée**.
4. **Le garçon** tient **le cerf-volant**.
5. Le cygne nage sur **le lac**.
6. Maman est sur **le banc**.
7. **L'enfant** court vers sa maman.

1. **The girl** is on **the swing**.
2. William and Annie are on **the see-saw**.
3. There is a dog on **the path**.
4. **The boy** is holding **the kite**.
5. The swan is swimming on **the lake**.
6. Mum is on **the bench**.
7. **The child** is running towards his mum.

la fille
lah fee

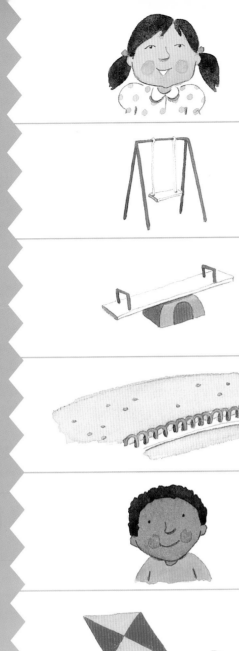

la balançoire

lah balon-swah

la balançoire

lah balon-swah

l'allée

lal-eh

le garçon

ler gar-soh

le cerf-volant

ler sair-voloh

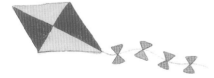

le lac

ler lack

le banc

ler boh

l'enfant

lonfoh

9

Jouons! - Let's play!

1	Les équipes jouent au **football**.	1	The teams are playing **football**.
2	Mes amis jouent au **ping-pong**.	2	My friends are playing **table tennis**.
3	Mon père aime **faire du ski**.	3	My father likes **skiing**.
4	Mon frère **pêche** dans le lac.	4	My brother **is fishing** in the lake.
5	Ma sœur est bonne en **gymnastique**.	5	My sister is good at **gymnastics**.
6	Marc est bon en **athlétisme**.	6	Mark is good at **athletics**.
7	Ma mère **fait du vélo**.	7	My mother **is cycling**.
8	Je **nage** tous les jours.	8	I **swim** every day.
9	Les garçons jouent au **basket**.	9	The boys are playing **basketball**.

le football

ler foot<u>bol</u>

le ping-pong

ler peeng-<u>pong</u>

faire du ski

fair-doo-<u>skee</u>

pêcher

peh-<u>shay</u>

la gymnastique

lah jeem-nass-<u>teek</u>

l'athlétisme

lat-leh-<u>tees</u>-m

faire du vélo

fair doo <u>vay</u>lo

nager

nah-<u>shay</u>

le basket

ler bas<u>ket</u>

En ville - In town

1	**L'école** a un toit vert.		1	**The school** has a green roof.
2	Il y a **une maison** blanche au coin de la rue.		2	There is **a** white **house** on the corner of the street.
3	Le train quitte **la gare**.		3	The train is leaving **the station**.
4	**La poste** est derrière **le supermarché**.		4	**The post office** is behind **the supermarket**.
5	Il y a beaucoup **de magasins**.		5	There are lots of **shops**.
6	**L'usine** est très grande.		6	**The factory** is very big.
7	Il y a la queue **au cinéma**.		7	There is a queue at **the cinema**.
8	**Le marché** est plein de monde.		8	**The market** is very busy.

l'école

leh-<u>kol</u>

la maison

lah may-<u>zoh</u>

la gare

lah gaar

la poste

lah post

le supermarché

ler soo-pair-marsh-<u>ay</u>

le magasin

ler mag-ah-<u>zah</u>

l'usine

l'yoo-<u>zeen</u>

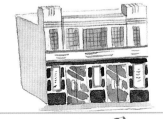

le cinéma

ler see-nay-<u>mah</u>

le marché

ler mar-<u>shay</u>

13

Au supermarché – At the supermarket

1	Il n'y a pas de **pain**!	1	There's no **bread**!
2	**Les œufs** sont cassés.	2	**The eggs** are broken.
3	Le chien vole **la viande**.	3	The dog is stealing **the meat**.
4	L'homme coupe **le poisson**.	4	The man is cutting **the fish**.
5	**Le riz** est à côté **des pâtes**.	5	**The rice** is next to **the pasta**.
6	**Le beurre** est cher.	6	**The butter** is expensive.
7	Le chat boit **le lait**.	7	The cat is drinking **the milk**.
8	Maman achète **du sucre**.	8	Mum is buying **sugar**.

le pain

ler pah

l'œuf

lerf

la viande

lah vee-ond

le poisson

ler pwah-son

le riz

ler ree

les pâtes

leh pat

le beurre

ler ber

le lait

ler lay

le sucre

ler s'yoo-kr'

Acheter des fruits - Buying fruit

1	**Les pommes** sont vertes.	1	**The apples** are green.
2	La femme mange **une pêche**.	2	The woman is eating **a peach**.
3	Il y a beaucoup de **cerises**.	3	There are lots of **cherries**.
4	**Les oranges** sont juteuses.	4	**The oranges** are juicy.
5	**L'ananas** est énorme!	5	**The pineapple** is huge!
6	**Les mangues** sont délicieuses.	6	**Mangoes** are delicious.
7	L'enfant lance **la banane**.	7	The child is throwing **the banana**.
8	L'oiseau veut **les raisins**.	8	The bird wants **the grapes**.
9	**Les fraises** sont rouges.	9	**The strawberries** are red.

la pomme

lah pom

la pêche

la pesh

la cerise

lah seh-reez

l'orange

loronsh

l'ananas

lan-an-ah

la mangue

lah mon-ger

la banane

lah ban-an

les raisins

leh ray-zah

la fraise

lah frairz

Acheter des vêtements - Shopping for clothes

1	Le chapeau est trop **grand**.	1	The hat is too **big**.
2	La robe est trop **petite**.	2	The dress is too **small**.
3	L'écharpe est trop **longue**.	3	The scarf is too **long**.
4	Le pantalon est trop **court**.	4	The trousers are too **short**.
5	Le manteau est **cher**.	5	The coat is **expensive**.
6	La robe est **jolie**.	6	The dress is **pretty**.
7	La petite fille est **heureuse**.	7	The little girl is **happy**.
8	Le petit garçon est **triste**.	8	The little boy is **sad**.
9	La glace est **bonne**.	9	The ice-cream is **good**.

grand/grande

groh/grond

petit/petite

p'-tee/p'-teet

long/longue

loh/lon-ger

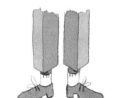

court/courte

kor/kort

cher/chère

share/share

joli/jolie

shol-ee/shol-ee

heureux/heureuse

er-er/er-erz

triste

treest

bon/bonne

boh/bon

19

Quel temps fait-il? - What's the weather like?

1	**Le soleil** brille à la plage.	1	**The sun** is shining at the beach.
2	**Il fait chaud**.	2	**It's hot**.
3	Mais **il pleut** sur la colline.	3	But **it's raining** on the hill.
4	Et **les nuages** sont gris.	4	And **the clouds** are grey.
5	Et **le vent** est fort.	5	And **the wind** is strong.
6	Il y a **un orage** magnifique!	6	There is a magnificent **storm**!
7	Sur la mer il y a **du brouillard**.	7	On the sea there is **fog**.
8	Dans les montagnes **il fait froid** et **il neige**!	8	In the mountains **it's cold** and **it's snowing**!

le soleil

ler sol-ay

il fait chaud

eel fay show

il pleut

eel pler

le nuage

ler noo-ah-sh

le vent

ler voh

l'orage

lor-ah-sh

le brouillard

ler brwee-ar

il fait froid

eel fay frwah

il neige

eel nair-sh

L'année - The year

1	Il y a quatre **saisons**.	1	There are four **seasons**.
2	J'aime **le printemps**.	2	I like **spring**.
3	En **mars** il y a du vent.	3	**March** is windy.
4	Il pleut souvent en **avril**.	4	It often rains in **April**.
5	Il y a beaucoup de fleurs en **mai**.	5	There are lots of flowers in **May**.
6	**L'été**, je vais en vacances.	6	In the **summer**, I go on holiday.
7	La fleur de **juin**, c'est la rose.	7	**June**'s flower is the rose.
8	L'anniversaire de mon ami est en **juillet.**	8	My friend's birthday is in **July**.
9	Il fait chaud en **août**.	9	It's hot in **August**.

la saison

lah say-zoh

le printemps

ler pran-toh

mars

marss

avril

av-reel

mai

may

l'été

leh-tay

juin

sh-wah

juillet

shwee-ay

août

oot

L'année - The year

1 **L'automne** commence en **septembre**.	1 **Autumn** starts in **September**.
2 En **octobre**, les feuilles tombent.	2 In **October** the leaves fall.
3 En Australie, il fait chaud en **novembre**.	3 In Australia, it's hot in **November**.
4 En **décembre**, il y a Noël!	4 Christmas is in **December**!
5 **L'hiver** amène de la neige!	5 **Winter** brings snow.
6 En **janvier**, il fait froid.	6 It is cold in **January**.
7 **Février** est le mois du Carnaval.	7 **February** is Carnival month.
8 Il y a douze **mois** dans l'année.	8 There are twelve **months** in the year.

l'automne

lot-on

septembre

sep-tom-br'

octobre

ok-tobr'

novembre

no-vom-br'

l'hiver

lee-vair

décembre

deh-som-br'

janvier

shon-vee-ay

février

feh-vree-ay

le mois

ler mwah

Cultiver des légumes - Growing vegetables

1 Il y a huit **pommes de terre**.	1 There are eight **potatoes**.
2 **Le maïs** est jaune.	2 **The corn** is yellow.
3 **Les carottes** ont des feuilles vertes.	3 **The carrots** have green leaves.
4 **Les choux** sont ronds.	4 **The cabbages** are round.
5 **Les courgettes** et **les aubergines** sont grosses.	5 **The courgettes** and **the aubergines** are big.
6 **Les tomates** et **le céleri** sont dans le panier.	6 **The tomatoes** and **the celery** are in the basket.
7 Les bestioles mangent **les laitues**.	7 The pests are eating **the lettuces**.

la pomme de terre

lah pom der <u>tair</u>

le maïs

ler mah-<u>eess</u>

la carotte

la kah-<u>rot</u>

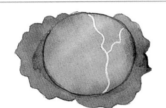

le chou

ler shoo

la courgette

lah kor-<u>shet</u>

l'aubergine

loh-bair-<u>sheen</u>

la tomate

lah to-<u>mat</u>

la laitue

lah layt-<u>yoo</u>

le céleri

ler sel-air-<u>ee</u>

Dans le forêt - In the forest

1	**Le renard** a une longue queue.	1	**The fox** has a long tail.
2	**L'écureuil** est sur la branche.	2	**The squirrel** is on the branch.
3	**Le cerf** mange des feuilles.	3	**The deer** is eating leaves.
4	Où est **l'ours brun?**	4	Where is **the brown bear**?
5	**Le lapin** court vers son terrier.	5	**The rabbit** runs into its burrow.
6	Il y a beaucoup **de papillons**.	6	There are lots of **butterflies**.
7	**Les scarabées** sont noirs.	7	**The beetles** are black.
8	**La chenille** est sur la feuille.	8	**The caterpillar** is on the leaf.
9	**Les mouches** sont énervantes!	9	**The flies** are annoying!

le renard
ler ren-ar

l'écureuil
leh-koorer-yee

le cerf
ler sair

l'ours brun
loorss-bruh

le lapin
ler lah-pah

le papillon
ler papee-oh

le scarabée
ler skah-rah-bay

la chenille
lah sher-nee-yer

la mouche
lah moosh

Questions - Questions

1	**Qui** est cet homme?	1	**Who** is that man?
2	**Qu'est-ce que** c'est?	2	**What**'s that?
3	**Quand** est-ce que vous fermez?	3	**When** do you shut?
4	**Où** sont mes lunettes?	4	**Where** are my glasses?
5	**Pourquoi** rit-il?	5	**Why** is he laughing?
6	**Comment** on dit "chien"?	6	**How** do you say 'dog'?
7	Ça coûte **combien**?	7	**How much** does it cost?
8	Il a **combien** d'animaux?	8	**How many** animals does he have?
9	**Je peux** vous aider?	9	**Can I** help you?

qui?

kee

qu'est-ce que?

kess-ker

quand?

koh

où?

ooh

pourquoi?

poor-kwah

comment?

kom-oh

combien?

kom-bee-ah

combien?

kom-bee-ah

je peux?

sh per

31

Word list

Ma maison p.2 — **My house**
Les pièces de la maison — **Rooms of the house**

la chambre	bedroom
la cuisine	kitchen
l'escalier	stairs
le jardin	garden
le plafond	ceiling
la salle de bain	bathroom
le salon	sitting room
les toilettes	toilet
le toit	roof

Pendant la semaine p.4 — **During the week**
Les jours de la semaine — **Days of the week**

lundi	Monday
mardi	Tuesday
mercredi	Wednesday
jeudi	Thursday
vendredi	Friday
samedi	Saturday
dimanche	Sunday
aujourd'hui	today
demain	tomorrow

Visiter un ami p.6 — **Visiting a friend**
Expressions utiles — **Useful expressions**

au revoir	goodbye
bonjour	hello
ça va	that's okay
merci	thanks
non	no
oui	yes
pardon	sorry
s'il vous plaît	please
voilà	here you are

Au parc p.8 — **At the park**
Le parc — **The park**

l'allée	path
la balançoire	swing
la balançoire	see-saw
le banc	bench
le cerf-volant	kite
l'enfant	child
la fille	girl
le garçon	boy
le lac	lake

Jouons! p.10 — **Let's play!**
Le sport — **Sports**

l'athlétisme	athletics
le basket	basketball
faire du ski	skiing
faire du vélo	cycling
le football	football
la gymnastique	gymnastics
nager	swimming
pêcher	fishing
le ping-pong	table tennis

En ville p.12 — **In town**
La ville — **The town**

le cinéma	cinema
l'école	school
la gare	station
le magasin	shop
la maison	house
le marché	market
la poste	post office
le supermarché	supermarket
l'usine	factory

Au supermarché p.14 — **At the supermarket**
Le supermarché — **The supermarket**

le beurre	butter
le lait	milk
l'œuf	egg
le pain	bread
les pâtes	pasta
le poisson	fish
le riz	rice
le sucre	sugar
la viande	meat

Acheter des fruits p.16 — **Buying fruit**
Les fruits — **Fruit**

l'ananas	pineapple
la banane	banana
la cerise	cherry
la fraise	strawberry
la mangue	mango
l'orange	orange
la pêche	peach
la pomme	apple
les raisins	grapes

Acheter des vêtements p.18 — **Shopping for clothes**
Les adjectifs — **Adjectives**

joli/jolie	pretty
bon/bonne	good
cher/chère	expensive
court/courte	short
grand/grande	big
heureux/heureuse	happy
long/longue	long
petit/petite	small
triste	sad

Quel temps fait-il? p.20 — **What's the weather like?**
Le temps — **Weather**

le brouillard	fog
il fait chaud	it's hot
il fait froid	it's cold
il neige	it's snowing
le nuage	cloud
l'orage	storm
il pleut	it's raining
le soleil	sun
le vent	wind

L'année p.22 — **The year**
Le printemps et l'été — **Spring and summer**

la saison	season
le printemps	spring
mars	March
avril	April
mai	May
l'été	summer
juin	June
juillet	July
août	August

L'année p.24 — **The year**
L'automne et l'hiver — **Autumn and winter**

l'automne	autumn
septembre	September
octobre	October
novembre	November
l'hiver	winter
décembre	December
janvier	January
février	February
le mois	month

Cultiver des légumes p.26 — **Growing vegetables**
Les légumes — **Vegetables**

l'aubergine	aubergine
la carotte	carrot
le céleri	celery
le chou	cabbage
la courgette	courgette
la laitue	lettuce
le maïs	corn
la pomme de terre	potato
la tomate	tomato

Dans la forêt p.28 — **In the forest**
Les animaux et les insectes — **Animals and insects**

le cerf	deer
la chenille	caterpillar
l'écureuil	squirrel
le lapin	rabbit
la mouche	fly
l'ours brun	brown bear
le papillon	butterfly
le renard	fox
le scarabée	beetle

Questions p.30 — **Questions**
Questions — **Questions**

combien?	how many?
combien?	how much?
comment?	how?
où?	where?
pourquoi?	why?
je peux?	can I?
quand?	when?
qu'est-ce que?	what?
qui?	who?